The
TREASURE
PRINCIPLE
BIBLE STUDY

REVISED AND UPDATED

BRIAN SMITH
&
RANDY ALCORN

MULTNOMAH

THE TREASURE PRINCIPLE BIBLE STUDY

All Scripture quotations, unless otherwise indicated, are taken from the Holy Bible, New International Version®, NIV®. Copyright © 1973, 1978, 1984 by Biblica Inc.® Used by permission. All rights reserved worldwide.

Italics in Scripture notations reflect the author's added emphasis.

Trade Paperback ISBN 978-1-59052-620-0

Copyright © 2003, 2018 by Eternal Perspective Ministries

Cover image by Getty Images/David Aubrey

Published in the United States by Multnomah, an imprint of the Crown Publishing Group, a division of Penguin Random House LLC, New York. Originally published in the United States in slightly different form by Multnomah, an imprint of the Crown Publishing Group, a division of Penguin Random House LLC, New York, in 2003.

MULTNOMAH® and its mountain colophon are trademarks of Penguin Random House LLC.

Printed in the United States of America

30 29 28 27 26 25 24 23 22 21

SPECIAL SALES
Most Multnomah books are available at special quantity discounts when purchased in bulk by corporations, organizations, and special-interest groups. Custom imprinting or excerpting can also be done to fit special needs. For information, please e-mail specialmarketscms@penguinrandomhouse.com or call 1-800-603-7051.

Contents

Note to Readers from Randy Alcorn . . . . *iv*

Introduction: The Joyous Paradox . . . . *v*

LESSON 1
Welcome to the Paradigm of Grace and Joy! *1*

LESSON 2
Gaining Wealth That Matters *7*

LESSON 3
Tangible Treasures *13*

LESSON 4
Owner or Manager? *19*

LESSON 5
Giving—A Gift to Ourselves *25*

LESSON 6
Redirecting Our Eyes *31*

LESSON 7
Redirecting Our Hearts *39*

LESSON 8
The Sojourner's Mindset *45*

LESSON 9
Treasure Now or Later? *53*

LESSON 10
Learning to Give *59*

LESSON 11
Good Question... . . . . *67*

LESSON 12
Catch the Vision *73*

LESSON 13
Prepare for Action *79*

Note to Readers from Randy Alcorn

After studying *The Treasure Principle,* my friend Brian Smith wrote most of the questions in this book. My part was to go over those questions, revise them, cut some, and add others. So...I wrote *The Treasure Principle;* Brian wrote the first draft of this study guide; then I made additions and changes. Brian did most of the work on this guide, and I want to make sure he gets the credit. Both of us want to thank Doug Gabbert and Jay Echternach of Multnomah Publishers, who saw the need for this study guide. Thanks also to our editor, Jennifer Gott. And thanks above all to our Lord Jesus, who though He was rich, yet for our sakes became poor, that we through His poverty might become rich.

THE JOYOUS PARADOX

Die to live.

Mourn to rejoice.

Impoverish to abound.

Bow down to be raised up.

Lose to gain.

Give to receive.

These are all part of the same truth: Whatever we give to God, He will return to us many times over, both for His glory and for our good.

God offers us His greatest gift...Himself. With Him comes a life full of joy and purpose. We were made for a person and a place. Jesus is the person. Heaven is the place.

But we're not yet home in heaven. Why the wait? Because God has work for us to do on earth, work for which He empowers us—the work of giving away our lives, including our wealth, for the sake of the needy and for the glory of God.

This Bible study, a companion to Randy Alcorn's *The Treasure Principle,* can help you learn what it means to invest in eternity—to live and give now in a way that will pay off forever.

ROYAL PILGRIMS

On your journey through this foreign land called earth, as you make your way toward home, you are not alone. Our Father's intention is for us to travel with others.

Your journey through this Bible study will be most profitable, and the changes in your life most lasting, if you walk beside someone else.

You can certainly profit from a self-study, but if you're not planning to join with a partner or group, consider it.

The Treasure Principle is a powerful little book because it conveys life-changing truths from Scripture that show us God's way to joy, both here and in eternity. This companion Bible study supplements the book by examining the same truths from a different approach. Here you will slow down and digest, one at a time, the ingredients of Christ's Treasure Principle. Maybe you're not yet convinced.... Maybe you're onboard, but you wish to lay the building blocks.... Maybe you're enthusiastic—this study will reinforce and fine-tune your insights.

WHAT CAN I EXPECT?

Personal Connection with God

The Treasure Principle Bible Study guides you to Christ, our central treasure. Only in His presence can you make the changes in thinking and behavior that the Treasure Principle requires. Only in His power and grace can you find the joy of obedience.

Keep a Bible beside you. You'll refer to it frequently, unearthing nuggets of truth, discovering God's heart. He doesn't promise that our words—or those of any man—won't return empty, but He does promise that *His* words won't return without accomplishing their purpose (Isaiah 55:11).

Randy's desire is that readers of all his books, including *The Treasure Principle*, would be guided by this example: "Now the Bereans were of more noble character than the Thessalonians, for they received the message with great eagerness and examined the Scriptures every day to see if what Paul said was true" (Acts 17:11).

Mutual Support with Other People

This study is designed for personal reflection followed by discussion with a partner or group. Any of the questions in the study can serve as the basis for discussion, but you'll find in each lesson several questions written specifically for dialogue between you and others. In a group, select some of the personal study questions for discussion, then supplement them with some added discussion questions ("For Further Discussion")—whichever you determine to be best for your group. The goal is to have is a profitable discussion, *not* to address every question.

Integrated Wisdom from The Treasure Principle

Short quotations from *The Treasure Principle* are sown throughout each lesson, seeds of wisdom that will grow in you as you consider them more deeply. Even a person who's never read *The Treasure Principle* could glean its central points through the selections included here. Of course, since this guide closely follows the book, you'll benefit most by reading the designated portion of *The Treasure Principle* before doing each lesson.

Honesty Before God

Lessons also include "Questions for God" that prompt you to honestly approach the Lord with uncertainties, fears, joys, and new discoveries. An open examination of your heart before God, together with a genuine desire for His guidance, will free you to deal with issues you might otherwise suppress. Facing such issues will encourage you to do the right things for the right reasons rather than settling into superficial performance. God is interested not only in the recipients of our giving, but in the work of grace He does *in us* through our giving.

God's Truth in Your Heart

In "For Meditation and Memorization," you'll be encouraged to take to heart one short Scripture passage. *Meditation* is first because as you absorb the meaning and implications of God's Word, it abides in your heart. We encourage you to write the passage from each lesson on a card and carry it with you during the week. Don't worry about trying to memorize it immediately. Simply read it several times each day, pray over it, ponder its meaning, and consider its implications for you. When you have done this for several days, you'll likely find the words embedded in your heart. You may memorize it without even trying.

WHAT WILL IT TAKE?

You need not start this study fully convinced or thoroughly committed. Working through this study may be a pilgrimage as you thoughtfully weigh God's commands, invitations, teachings, and promises. You'll find yourself challenged to consider choices at the forks in life's path. So begin your journey with a desire to learn—and to trust God to work within you.

Determine to set aside the cynicism that life experiences may have cultivated in you. Open your ears again to God's promises...promises of hope and joy. Set aside the ugly stereotypes of religious hucksters trying to part fools from their money. This study is not about drudgery or legalism. It's about joy and freedom. This study is not designed to impose guilt, but to open wide doors of opportunity for eternal investment.

Our miracle-working God does mighty works in those who trust His words. Are you willing to invest some time and effort, with potential returns that are out of this world? Then this study is for you!

WELCOME TO THE PARADIGM OF GRACE AND JOY!

Based on the introduction (pages xv–xvi)
and pages 1–5 of chapter 1, "Buried Treasure" in
The Treasure Principle, Revised and Updated

You are about to contemplate what may be a very different way of thinking, a new perspective on life and eternity. It's a paradigm of grace and joy. The evil one is a liar who attempts to hide and distort the truth (John 8:43–44). Please ask your Father now to protect you and guide you into His truth.

THE PROMISE AND THE PROBLEM

Few people, even Bible-believing Christians, grasp the incredible joy available through God's grace. We squander vast resources in our quest for joy, trying to buy happiness. But it never works. And all the while, delight is within our grasp. According to Jesus, we gain joy in ways that are paradoxical and counterintuitive. We gain what will last only by giving up what won't.

> All your life, you've been on a treasure hunt. You've been searching for a perfect person and a perfect place. Jesus is that person; heaven is that place. So if you're a Christian,

you've already met the person, and you're already headed to the place.

But there's a problem. You're not yet living with that person, and you're not yet living in that place!

1. Take a moment to consider your life dreams. Consider how often many people move from relationship to relationship and home to home. What are they looking for? Can you see the choices people (and you) make in terms of a quest for the perfect person and the perfect place?

2. How have "reason" and "practicality" tempted you to downplay the joy Christ offers, or to pursue it less passionately?

Some books try to motivate giving out of guilt. This isn't one of them. This book is about something else—the joy of giving.

3. What do you hope to gain from this study?

The Life-Changing Discovery

4. Read Matthew 13:44, the parable of the hidden treasure. In what ways are you like this fortunate man? In what ways are you different? (All parables should be read in light of their central point, so focus on the man's consuming joy in finding his treasure, not on the ethical question of whether it would be right not to tell the landowner he found it.)

5. Randy uses Matthew 13:44 to emphasize the joy that comes from finding and investing in treasure (recognizing that true treasures are eternal, unlike the sort found in the field). Matthew 6:19–21 and 1 Timothy 6:18–19 describe giving as storing up treasures in heaven. 2 Corinthians 8:2 and 9:7 connect giving with joy and cheerfulness. Do you recall some times when you found particular joy in giving?

From the moment of his discovery, the traveler's life changes. The treasure captures his imagination, becomes the stuff of his dreams. It's his reference point, his new center of gravity. The traveler takes every new step with this treasure in mind. He experiences a radical paradigm shift.

6. Imagine valuing God's kingdom the way this traveler valued his newly discovered treasure. What would your life be like?

7. What would it take for you to find such joy in life? Would it be worth parting with money and things to obtain it?

Talk with your Father about both your longings and His. Share honestly with Him any obstacles that stand between you and the life of joy. Invite His help in overcoming those obstacles. Thank Him in faith for His answers, which will bring you joy.

THE MONEY CONNECTION

Why did Jesus put such an emphasis on money and possessions?

Because there's a fundamental connection between our spiritual lives and how we think about and handle money. We may try to divorce our faith and our finances, but God sees them as inseparable.

I realized that our approach to money and possessions isn't just important—it's central to our spiritual lives.

8. How do the following passages show the connection between our spiritual lives and how we handle money and possessions?

- Matthew 2:11

- Luke 3:8–14

- Luke 19:8–10

- Deuteronomy 26:10–11

- 2 Chronicles 29:31–33

QUESTIONS FOR GOD

Ask the following questions to God in prayer if they represent your heart. Write down the responses He may give through Scripture and your sense of His personal leading.

9. *God, how can I find the joy You promise? How can I risk pursuing Your joy with my whole heart?*

10. *How well am I expressing love for You, love for others, and the pursuit of true joy through how I handle the money and possessions You've entrusted to my care?*

FOR MEDITATION AND MEMORIZATION

"The kingdom of heaven is like treasure hidden in a field.

When a man found it, he hid it again,

and then in his joy went and sold all

he had and bought that field."

MATTHEW 13:44

FOR FURTHER DISCUSSION

1. The God of all creation and of all possibilities has promised joy beyond our comprehension (Psalm 16:11; John 15:10–11; Galatians 5:22). Let's allow our imaginations to soar. What might living in God's joy be like?

2. How have you seen believers—perhaps yourself—searching for joy in the wrong places?

3. What decisions and attitudes will allow you to experience the joy God promises in Matthew 13:44?

4. Describe a situation you have seen or experienced—positive or negative—in which the connection between spirituality and handling of material wealth was evident.

5. How can we remind ourselves of this connection? How can we encourage each other toward the joy of giving (Hebrews 10:24)?

Lesson 2

GAINING WEALTH
THAT MATTERS

Based on pages 5–12 of chapter 1, "Buried Treasure,"
in *The Treasure Principle, Revised and Updated*

Jesus offers you great joy, both now and eternally, as you bring Him glory through your choices. Take a moment to invite Him to work within you so that your heart might beat with His desires.

Have you chosen a partner or group for your journey through these lessons? By yourself you can certainly gain much from this study, but the likelihood that you will grow in deep and lasting ways improves dramatically when you travel in company. Who will you take with you?

WISELY WEIGHING THE FUTURE

Using our material wealth according to eternal values is certainly a matter of morality. It's right. But it is also a matter of *wisdom*—it's smart.

> Do you feel sorry for the traveler [of Matthew 13:44]? After all, his discovery cost him everything. But we aren't to pity this man; we're to *envy* him! His sacrifice pales in comparison to his reward....
>
> The traveler made short-term sacrifices to obtain a long-term reward. "It cost him everything he owned," you might lament. Yes, *but it gained him everything that mattered.*
>
> If we miss the phrase "in his joy," we miss everything.

The man wasn't exchanging lesser treasures for greater treasures out of dutiful drudgery but out of joyful exhilaration. He would have been a fool not to do exactly what he did.

1. Read Matthew 13:44 and 19:16–26. Complete the following chart comparing the two men:

	THE TRAVELER	THE RICH YOUNG MAN
Amount invested		
Change in wealth		
Emotional state after decision		

2. What decisions might God be challenging you to make in order to experience the traveler's joy? (Take a moment to ask Him for insight.)

Consider what Jesus is saying [in Matthew 6:19–21]: "Do not store up for yourselves treasures on earth." Why not? Because earthly treasures are bad? No. *Because they won't last.*

3. What dangers arise when we forget the limitations of material wealth (Luke 16:13–15; 1 Timothy 6:9–10)?

4. In what sense is our money like Confederate currency (*The Treasure Principle, Revised and Updated*, 7–8)? If we viewed it that way, how would our financial strategies and giving be affected?

ENLIGHTENED SELF-INTEREST

God intends our obedience to be motivated not only by His glory and the good of others, but also by our own good.

> Jesus has a treasure mentality. He *wants* us to store up treasures. He's just telling us to stop storing them in the wrong place and start storing them in the right place!
>
> "Store up *for yourselves*." Doesn't it seem strange that Jesus commands us to do what's in our own best interests? Wouldn't that be selfish? No. God expects and commands us to act out of enlightened self-interest. He wants us to live to His glory, but what is to His glory is always to our good....
>
> Selfishness is when we pursue gain at the expense of others. But...it is by serving God and others that we store up heavenly treasures. Everyone gains; no one loses.

5. Why can the motivation encouraged by Matthew 19:29–30 be considered a healthy way of thinking?

6. According to Philippians 3:7–14, how can we view even Paul's sacrifice as motivated by not only God's glory and others' good, but also his own self-interest?

7. Explain this statement from *The Treasure Principle:* "Present joy comes from anticipating future joy."

Reflect before your Father on your values and assumptions. It's safe to share honestly with Him. Consider which of your heart's affections are truly in His and your best interests and which might be harmful. Thank Him for any truthful insight He provides—it's for your good and His glory.

INVESTING IN JOY, PRESENT AND FUTURE

Jesus said, "Store up for yourselves treasures in heaven, where moth and rust do not destroy, and where thieves do not break in and steal" (Matthew 6:20).

8. Agree or disagree? "Christ's stated reason for storing up treasures in heaven is simply because it's the right thing to do." Explain.

This is the Treasure Principle: "You can't take it with you—but you *can* send it on ahead."

9. How can you "send it on ahead"?

10. How does each of these passages relate to the Treasure Principle?

   • Psalm 49:16–17

   • 1 Timothy 6:17–19

QUESTIONS FOR GOD

Raise these questions before your Father, and note any responses He provides through His Word, your conscience, or wise fellow believers.

11. *How can I achieve full confidence that what You want—and what You command—is always for my good?*

12. *Why do I want to hold on to my wealth, even the part I don't need? Is it pride? Selfishness? Insecurity? Fear? Or is it a desire for control? Power? Prestige? Am I trying to prove something? What am I trying to prove? And to whom? Or am I just going with the flow of my culture because it's easier? How can I change, Lord?*

FOR MEDITATION AND MEMORIZATION

"But store up for yourselves treasures in heaven,

where moth and rust do not destroy,

and where thieves do not break in and steal.

For where your treasure is, there your heart will be also."

MATTHEW 6:20–21

FOR FURTHER DISCUSSION

1. How have you experienced the genuine value of earthly wealth? How have you encountered the limitations of earthly wealth?
2. Describe specific ways in which you or others you know have stored up treasure in heaven by godly use of treasure on earth (Matthew 6:19–21).
3. Explain some of the fantasies and falsehoods the world would like us to believe about material wealth.
4. With whom might you share your excitement about the Treasure Principle? How might you best convey a passion for giving?

TANGIBLE TREASURES

Based on pages 13–21 of chapter 2, "Was Jesus Really Talking About
Financial Giving?" in *The Treasure Principle, Revised and Updated*

This chapter was added to the revised and updated version of *The
Treasure Principle* in response to claims that Jesus was talking about
something other than financial giving when He gave instructions about
storing up treasures in Heaven.

WHAT IS MEANT BY "TREASURES IN HEAVEN"?

1. Some have said "treasures in Heaven" can't be tangible because
   Heaven is not tangible. How would you counter that claim using
   these passages?

   • Matthew 25:21, 23

   • John 14:2

   • 1 Thessalonians 4:13–18

- Revelation 21:3

- Revelation 22:3

We don't know the exact form the treasures in Heaven will take. Randy says, "Treasures in Heaven could be of material or spiritual nature, but either way they are real, meaningful rewards for God's people who give generously." Consider the array of things for which we are promised eternal rewards:

- **Doing good works:** "Because you know that *the Lord will reward everyone for whatever good he does,* whether he is slave or free" (Ephesians 6:8) and *"God 'will give to each person according to what he has done'...*glory, honor and peace for everyone who does good: first for the Jew, then for the Gentile" (Romans 2: 6, 10).

- **Persevering under persecution:** "Blessed are you when men hate you, when they exclude you and insult you and reject your name as evil, because of the Son of Man. Rejoice in that day and leap for joy, because great is your reward in heaven. For that is how their fathers treated the prophets" (Luke 6:22–23).

- **Showing compassion to the needy:** "But when you give a banquet, invite the poor, the crippled, the lame, the blind, and you will be blessed. Although they cannot repay you, you will be repaid at the resurrection of the righteous" (Luke 14:13–14).

- **Treating our enemies kindly:** "But love your enemies, do good to them, and lend to them without expecting to get anything back. Then *your reward will be great,* and you will be sons of the Most High, because he is kind to the ungrateful and wicked" (Luke 6:35).

2. Looking carefully at the italicized parts of these passages, which ones clearly corroborate the connection between treasures in Heaven and financial giving here on Earth? Explain your answer.

3. After considering these, along with other passages mentioned in chapter 2 of *The Treasure Principle,* do you agree with Randy's statement that treasures in Heaven "are real, meaningful rewards for God's people who give generously"? Why or why not?

4. Randy acknowledges Matthew 6:19–21 would be "far easier to fulfill if it merely required good intentions on our part. Instead, it calls us to radical acts of generosity." How might this help explain why some people prefer a more vague interpretation of "treasures in Heaven"? Explain your answer.

5. How does Paul's instruction to Timothy in 1 Timothy 6:18–19 strengthen the premise that Jesus is indeed talking about tangible, material generosity?

6. Now if someone told you Jesus wasn't talking about financial giving when He told us to "Store up for yourselves treasures in Heaven," how would you answer them?

QUESTIONS FOR GOD

If the following thoughts express your heart, raise them as prayers to God, and be ready to listen for His answers.

7. God, have I tried to put a spiritual spin on Your clear intentions about giving away material possessions, hoping to keep things vague so that I can maintain a comfortable lifestyle while still claiming to be "kingdom-minded"? Will You please show me any errors in my thinking about this so that together we can make the needed corrections?

8. If I truly believe "storing up treasures in Heaven means giving generously to kingdom causes and receiving God's rewards for doing so," what is it that You now want me to do? Will You help me choose obedience, even if what You're directing me toward is radically different from what I have been doing?

For Meditation and Memorization

"All these I have kept," the young man said.
"What do I still lack?" Jesus answered,
"If you want to be perfect, go, sell your possessions
and give to the poor, and you will have
treasure in heaven. Then come, follow me."

MATTHEW 19:20–21

FOR FURTHER DISCUSSION

1. The rich man of Matthew 6 was branded a fool for his greed; he continued to gather material wealth when he clearly had more than he could ever make use of himself. Describe examples you have seen, or participated in, of foolishly storing up treasures on Earth.

2. Share a personal story of someone blessing you by being "rich toward God" (Luke 12:21).

3. "Radical acts of generosity" may be easy to discuss. Putting them into action may be uncomfortable and should actually be quite costly. How can we help one another to be truly radical in the area of giving?

Lesson 4

OWNER OR
MANAGER?

Based on pages 22–30 of chapter 3, "Compounding Joy,"
in *The Treasure Principle, Revised and Updated*

This lesson's biblical principles are a solid foundation for your thinking
and living. They can also shake a faulty foundation on which you may
be building. Because some of your sources of security may be challenged, take a moment to ask your Father to grant you a sense of
security *in Him*. He is the solid rock on whom you can completely rely.

THE TITLE DEED TO THE UNIVERSE

At the root of our thinking about material wealth should be one truth
that is easy to understand yet difficult for many of us to accept: *God
owns everything*. His name, and His alone, is on the title deed to the
universe.

1. Picture your wealth—money, home, clothes, equipment, entertainment system...everything. Take several minutes to make sure you
   don't leave anything out, especially items you tend to take for
   granted. Now read the following passages. How closely does each
   passage line up with your thinking about your possessions?

- Deuteronomy 8:17–18

- 1 Chronicles 29:11–14

- Job 41:11

- 1 Corinthians 6:19–20

2. Why is it good that God owns our possessions and we don't?

Whenever we think like owners, it's a red flag.

3. List at least two dangers of assuming that we own our possessions.

THE HEART OF A STEWARD

If God's the owner, what's *our* role? Treasure Principle Key #1 says: "God owns everything. I'm His money manager."

4. In Matthew 25:14–30, what does Jesus teach about…

- God and possessions?

- people and possessions?

A steward manages assets for the owner's benefit. The
steward carries no sense of entitlement to the assets he
manages. It's his job to find out what the owner wants
done with his assets, then carry out his will.

5. What are some benefits in recognizing that we are stewards rather
   than owners?

6. Summarize God's instructions to you, whom He has trusted with
   the management of His wealth.

   - Luke 16:10–13

   - 1 Corinthians 4:2

Our name is on God's account. We have unrestricted
access to it, a privilege that is subject to abuse. As His
money managers, God trusts us to set our own salaries.
We draw needed funds from His wealth to pay our living
expenses. One of our central spiritual decisions is
determining what is a reasonable amount to live on...and
it will legitimately vary from person to person.

7. List two or three guidelines that can help you determine the "salary" you pay to yourself from God's wealth.

Take a moment now and talk with your Father about ownership and stewardship. Tell Him honestly the areas in which you find it hard to yield ownership to Him. Ask Him for eagerness to prove yourself a faithful steward.

JOYFUL GIVING

Thinking like a steward may not be easy at first, but it is guaranteed to bring great fulfillment. We were made to be stewards, and when we act like owners we invite stress, wrong perspectives, and destructive choices.

8. Observe the characteristics of the faithful stewards in Nehemiah 12:43 and Matthew 25:21, 23 (optional: Exodus 36:5–7; 2 Corinthians 8:2). How would your life be different if you lived like this more often?

"God loves a cheerful giver" (2 Corinthians 9:7). This doesn't mean we should give only when we're feeling cheerful. The cheerfulness often comes during and after the act of obedience, not before it.

9. When was the last time you gave yourself a chance to experience the fulfillment that comes with generous giving? How might you create such an opportunity in the next two weeks?

QUESTIONS FOR GOD

Consider directing the following questions toward God in prayer, especially if they represent questions that are already on your heart.

10. *God, am I treating You as owner and CEO of "my" assets, or am I treating You merely as my financial consultant, to whom at best I pay a fee in the form of offerings?*

11. *I'm frightened by the thought of giving up control of my things, even to You, God. What provision have You made to help me deal with these fears?*

FOR MEDITATION AND MEMORIZATION

Now it is required that those who have been given a trust must prove faithful.

1 CORINTHIANS 4:2

FOR FURTHER DISCUSSION

1. Share a fresh insight or reminder you have had about God's ownership as it relates to your possessions.
2. Which Scripture passages are most helpful in keeping you mindful of God's ownership and your stewardship?
3. Describe a situation you have seen or experienced in which faithful stewardship has been blessed or unwise stewardship has not.
4. Brainstorm a few strategies for changing your mindset from ownership to stewardship.
5. How can we help each other delight more fully in the joy and reward of faithful stewardship?

Lesson 5

GIVING—A GIFT
TO OURSELVES

Based on pages 30–38 of chapter 3, "Compounding Joy,"
in *The Treasure Principle, Revised and Updated*

God's grace is amazing. Grace was the manifestation of God's loving initiative toward us long before we ever did anything for Him. And it is both the model for and the power behind our giving. Stop and ask your Father to fill you with a deeper understanding and acceptance of His grace.

THE POWER OF GRACE
New Testament Greek uses closely related words for *grace* and *giving*. The word *grace* basically means "an undeserved gift."

1. Read Romans 5:6–21 and list several words and phrases describing what God's grace is and does.

2. Using these Scriptures as a guide, describe a few changes in our lives that are empowered by the grace of God.

- Acts 4:33

- Romans 6:14

- Romans 12:6–8

- 1 Corinthians 15:10

- 2 Corinthians 12:7–10

- 1 Peter 5:8–10

3. Write your own paraphrase of Titus 2:11–12, trying to capture Paul's meaning in terms that apply to your daily life today.

GRACE AND THE GIVER

Randy points out that "Christ's grace defines, motivates, and puts in perspective our giving." Just as God's grace guides and empowers all aspects of godly living, so also grace underpins the generosity of a wise steward. As Randy says, "As thunder follows lightning, giving follows grace."

4. Throughout 2 Corinthians 8–9, the themes of God's grace and our giving are intertwined. How does each of the following sections clarify the relationship between the two?

- 8:1–5

- 8:6–7

- 8:8–12

- 9:6–9

- 9:10–15

Gaze upon Christ long enough, and you'll become more of a giver. Give long enough, and you'll become more like Christ.

Our giving is a reflexive response to the grace of God in our lives.... This grace is the action; our giving is the reaction. We give because He first gave to us.

5. Take a few minutes to talk to your Father about His grace toward you. Write down a few of your possible responses to His grace—inward mental or emotional responses, and outward behavioral responses. How do these responses reveal ways that God's grace might impact your thinking, belief, and behavior?

THE FRINGE BENEFITS OF GIVING

God's grace alone should be motivation to give. But God is far more generous than we can conceive.

6. What does Isaiah 58:9–11 promise the generous giver? (Put your answer in terms of your life situation today.)

> Giving jump-starts our relationship with God. It opens our fists so we can receive what God has for us. When we see what it does for others and for us, we open our fists sooner and wider when the next chance comes.

7. Do you agree that giving jump-starts our relationship with God? If so, how?

8. How does Jeremiah 22:16 define "knowing God"?

Giving…breaks us out of orbit around our possessions.
We escape their gravity, entering a new orbit around our
treasures in heaven.

9. How does this change of "orbit" benefit the giver (1 John 2:15–17;
   also Matthew 6:19–21, 24)?

QUESTIONS FOR GOD

10. *Around what center does my life orbit: around things or around You?
    How can I make You more central to my thinking and living?*

11. *Do I really believe that You have made me to be a giver? Am I con-
    vinced that I will feel Your pleasure when I give? God, help me to
    believe and to trust You enough to give.*

FOR MEDITATION AND MEMORIZATION

And God is able to make all grace abound to you,
so that in all things at all times, having all that you need,
you will abound in every good work.

2 CORINTHIANS 9:8

FOR FURTHER DISCUSSION

1. What more can we learn about God's grace from Acts 20:32; Romans 3:22–24; Ephesians 1:4–8; 2:4–10; Hebrews 2:9; 4:15–16?
2. Describe an instance when you took a risky step of obedience because of God's grace.
3. What part does God's grace play in your motivation for giving? How can you become more intimately acquainted with His grace? How can we, your friends, help you do that?
4. What fringe benefits have you experienced as a result of giving?

REDIRECTING OUR EYES

Based on pages 39–44 of chapter 4, "Eyes on Eternity,"
in *The Treasure Principle, Revised and Updated*

A faithful steward of God's wealth needs a clear view of eternity. But our enemy tries to make us feel apprehensive, or at least apathetic, about heaven. Talk to your Father about your own view of eternity, asking Him to grant you understanding and eager anticipation.

HEAVEN, OUR TRUE HOME

If you imagine heaven as a place where you will strum a harp in endless tedium, you probably dread it. But if you trust Scripture, you will be filled with joy and excitement as you anticipate your heavenly home.

1. What reasons for excitement about eternity do these passages provide? (You won't find harps mentioned in any of them.)

   • Isaiah 25:6–9

   • John 14:2–3

- 1 Corinthians 6:2–3

- 2 Corinthians 4:17–18

- Revelation 21:1–4

- Revelation 22:1–5

2. Think about your impressions of heaven. If any of them seem negative or uninteresting to you, write them here. Then try to determine whether those impressions can be found in Scripture, either by searching the Bible yourself or by talking with your group, a Christian leader, or a friend who knows the Bible. (If you want to see how exciting Scripture shows heaven to be, see Randy Alcorn's *Heaven* [Carol Stream, IL: Tyndale, 2004]).

3. In light of Colossians 3:1–2, what do you think of the expression, "He's so heavenly minded he's of no earthly good"?

4. How would obedience to Colossians 3:1–2 affect your giving?

ETERNAL REWARD, OUR TRUE WEALTH

The essence of heaven is the very presence of God, which is far more wonderful than we can possibly comprehend now. In addition to the blessing of His presence, God will bestow unimaginable reward on us if we use our resources and opportunities on earth for Him.

5. What does each passage below teach about the nature of our reward and how we can earn it (some passages may not answer both questions)?

	NATURE OF ETERNAL REWARD	HOW WE CAN EARN REWARD
LUKE 6:35		
LUKE 14:12–14		
1 CORINTHIANS 3:8–15		
COLOSSIANS 3:23–24		
2 TIMOTHY 4:6–8		

6. List below a few actions you and others have taken that God might reward in heaven. How does your anticipation of this reward affect your attitude toward eternity?

> Jesus is keeping track of our smallest acts of kindness: "If
> anyone gives even a cup of cold water to one of these
> little ones because he is my disciple, I tell you the truth,
> he will certainly not lose his reward" (Matthew 10:42).

7. Think about the opportunities that surround you in your unique
sphere of influence. What one or two steps—large or small—could
you add to what you're already doing?

EXPANDING RESPONSIBILITY, OUR TRUE PURPOSE

One aspect of our reward for faithfulness and trustworthiness is that
God will entrust us with even greater opportunity, responsibility, and
authority, both on earth and in eternity.

8. According to each of these passages, how can giving make a difference in our lives?

• Matthew 19:21

• Luke 16:11–12

• Philippians 4:17

> By clinging to what isn't ours, we forgo the opportunity
> to be granted ownership in heaven. But by generously
> distributing God's property on earth, we will become
> property owners in heaven!

Giving is a giant lever positioned on the fulcrum of this world, allowing us to move mountains in the next world. Because we give, eternity will be different—for others and for us.

9. What greater responsibilities might God entrust you, on earth or in heaven, for your faithful management? How important is giving in this process of managing God's assets?

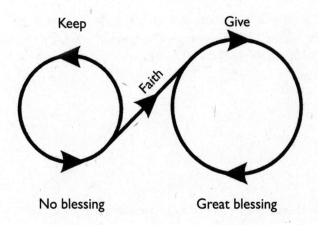

10. Consider the diagram above. Describe one active step of faith you would need to take in order to move from the left circle to the right circle.

11. What assurance do you have that God will safeguard you through this risky step of faith?

QUESTIONS FOR GOD

12. *Lord, how can I find the faith to set my eyes on the things I can't see (2 Corinthians 4:18)?*

13. *Am I living to hear others say of me, "He or she is a great success," or to hear You say, "Well done, my good and faithful servant"? Lord, help me to see You as the Audience of One and to live for Your approval, not the world's.*

FOR MEDITATION AND MEMORIZATION

Since, then, you have been raised with Christ,

set your hearts on things above,

where Christ is seated at the right hand of God.

Set your minds on things above, not on earthly things.

COLOSSIANS 3:1–2

For Further Discussion

1. What more can we learn about heaven and eternity from Matthew 8:11; Colossians 3:1–4; 2 Timothy 2:12; Hebrews 11:8–16, 24–26?
2. What additional insights might we discover regarding our eternal reward from Matthew 6:1–6; 10:41–42; Hebrews 10:32–36; 11:6; 1 Peter 1:3–5?
3. What thoughts about heaven and eternal reward are especially helpful to motivate you toward obedience?
4. Describe one small area of faithfulness in your life—or another's—that might lead to even greater responsibility later. How have you seen increased responsibility come out of past faithfulness?
5. How can we help each other keep our eyes fixed more firmly and accurately on eternity?

REDIRECTING OUR HEARTS

Based on pages 44–47 of chapter 4, "Eyes on Eternity,"
in *The Treasure Principle, Revised and Updated*

Randy writes, "As surely as the compass needle follows north, your heart will follow your treasure. Money leads; hearts follow." As you work through this lesson, ask your Father to strengthen your heart's affection toward Him.

GOD MADE US WITH STRONG DESIRES

We are emotional beings made in the image of a passionate God. God always directs His strong desires in righteous directions. As we grow in character, we will learn to aim our passions toward godly targets.

1. What healthy expressions of desire are represented in these passages?

   • Psalm 42:1–2

   • Proverbs 2:1–5

- Philippians 1:21–24

- Philippians 3:8–14

2. What is God's preference for the "temperature" of our passion (Revelation 3:15–16)? Why?

EAGER FOR ETERNAL REWARD?
We need to address a common misunderstanding.

Isn't it wrong to be motivated by reward? No, it isn't. If it were wrong, Christ wouldn't offer it to us as a motivation. Reward is His idea, not ours.

3. Read again a few of the Scripture passages in question 5 of lesson 5 (especially 1 Corinthians 3:8–15). What is God's purpose in promising us reward?

4. Who do you look forward to thanking in heaven? Who do you think might thank you for your prayers, and for giving of your time or money?

Do we deserve reward from God? No. We don't deserve a thing, and anything we receive is only because of His grace and love for us. But God has chosen to be a Father to us, and any loving father looks for ways to encourage behavior that pleases him. God's rewarding us for our obedience is simply good, loving parenting. He receives pleasure when we delight in our reward, as well as in the obedience that earns it. It may sound spiritual to say, "I don't care about reward," but it isn't—we should care about reward because God cares and wants us to care. That's why He talks so much about reward in His Word.

If desiring reward for obedience feels wrong to you, give yourself time to get used to these ideas. Both right behavior and the reward God has attached to it are expressions of His generous heart, so both are good. Talk to Him about your feelings, and invite Him to help you see and feel as He does.

WHERE WILL YOU AIM YOUR DESIRES?

Strong human passions are unavoidable—they're built into us by our Designer. Given that, we are responsible, in God's strength and wisdom, to choose how we exercise our passions. How is it that we direct our hearts? Treasure Principle Key #2 says, "My heart always goes where I put God's money."

5. According to Matthew 6:21, where should you place your treasure if you want to cultivate a heart for…

- recreation and hobbies?

- entertainment?

- retirement security?

- the world's lost, hungry, and persecuted?

- lost and needy people around you?

- ministry through your local church?

He who lays up treasures on earth spends his life backing away from his treasures. To him, death is loss.

He who lays up treasures in heaven looks forward to eternity; he's moving daily toward his treasures. To him, death is gain.

He who spends his life moving away from his treasures has reason to despair. He who spends his life moving toward his treasures has reason to rejoice.

6. Take a moment to consider how closely the preceding quote represents your own view. How does giving make us more joyful people?

7. Describe the treasure focus of each biblical figure portrayed in these passages:

- Acts 5:1–10

- Acts 7:55–60

- Hebrews 11:24–26

- Hebrews 12:2

8. Read Psalm 16:11; 27:4, 8; 37:4; and 73:23–28. Summarize the best central focus for our treasure and our hearts.

QUESTIONS FOR GOD

10. *As I move toward death, am I backing away from my treasure, or moving toward it? Am I living in despair, or in joyful anticipation?*

11. *I recognize the potential my passions and desires have to cause great harm or to achieve great good. God, will You help me direct my treasure and my passions toward You and Your eternal purposes?*

FOR MEDITATION AND MEMORIZATION

"For where your treasure is,
there your heart will be also."

MATTHEW 6:21

---- ❧ ----

FOR FURTHER DISCUSSION

1. How have you seen others, or yourself, attempt to stifle strong passions? Exploit passions? Channel passions without God's help? Submit passions to God?
2. How much is desire for eternal reward part of your motivation for giving? How can we help each other view eternal reward with a healthy attitude?
3. What do your checkbook, your credit card statements, your receipts, and your appointment book say about the placement of your treasure...and your heart?
4. How would you describe your attitude when giving? Is it a dispassionate act of philanthropy? Or do you give with immersion in God's kingdom causes? Or are you somewhere in between?
5. How personally connected with God do you feel? How does this affect your use of His money? Conversely, how might your giving enhance your sense of intimacy with your Father?

Lesson 8

THE SOJOURNER'S MINDSET

Based on pages 48–56 of chapter 5, "Roadblocks to Giving,"
in *The Treasure Principle, Revised and Updated*

What draws your heart toward heaven? What draws your heart toward earth? Spend a few minutes with your Father, pondering these questions and asking Him to help you see more clearly your citizenship in heaven and the fact that you are an alien, stranger, and pilgrim on earth.

AT HOME ON EARTH?

There are many roadblocks to giving: unbelief, insecurity, pride, idolatry, desire for power and control. The raging current of our culture—and often our churches—makes it hard to swim upstream. It's considered 'normal' to keep far more than we give.

But I'm convinced that the greatest deterrent to giving is this: the illusion that earth is our home.

1. Treasure Principle Key #3 says, "Heaven, not earth, is my home." What do each of the following passages tell us about this?

- Psalm 119:19

- Ephesians 2:19–22

- Philippians 3:20–21

- Hebrews 11:13–16

- 1 Peter 2:9–11

Paradoxically, our home is a place we've never been. But it's the place we were made for, the place made for us.

If we would let this reality sink in, it would forever change the way we think and live. We would stop laying up treasures in our earthly hotel rooms and start sending more ahead to our true home.

2. In what ways can we appreciate and use the good God has built into this foreign world while still keeping our eyes fixed on our true home in heaven?

3. Randy says we are here on a short-term visa that will soon expire. How would you live differently if you were in a country on a short-term visa rather than being a permanent resident?

4. Consider specifically the analogy of being a French citizen on a ninety-day sojourn in America, where you can earn money and send it back to France but can't take anything with you when you go home (*The Treasure Principle, Revised and Updated,* 49). No analogy is perfect, but is the central point of this one valid? If so, how should it affect our living and giving?

THE DOT AND THE LINE

Our present life on earth is the dot. It begins. It ends. It's brief. But from that dot extends a line that goes on forever. That line is eternity, which Christians will spend in heaven.

The Dot:
Life on earth

The Line:
Life in heaven

5. Moses, a man who lived 120 very full years, wrote Psalm 90. Read verses 1–12, and summarize his message in your own words.

6. What practical guidance does Scripture provide in keeping with Treasure Principle Key #4: "I should live not for the dot but for the line"?

- Psalm 103:13–18

- Isaiah 40:6–8

- James 1:9–12

- 1 Peter 1:3–5

The person who lives for the dot lives for treasures on earth that end up in junkyards. The person who lives for the line lives for treasures in heaven that will never end.
 Giving is living for the line.

Talk with your Father about your attitude toward heaven and earth—where your home is and what you're living for. If your assessment of your thinking is negative, accept the forgiveness God graciously offers (1 John 1:7, 9). He's eager to grant a fresh start to anyone who wants it. Begin to dream with Him about ways you can live for eternity *now*—and experience joy in the process.

POSSESSION OBSESSION

Ever seen that bumper sticker "He who dies with the most toys wins"?... The more accurate saying is "He who dies with the most toys still dies—and never takes his toys with him."

7. Describe at least two ways you are sometimes tempted to give in to the common misconception Jesus describes in Luke 12:15.

We think we own our possessions, but too often they own us.

Nothing makes a journey more difficult than a heavy backpack filled with nice but unnecessary things. Pilgrims travel light.

8. What kind of a master is material wealth (Matthew 6:24)? How does this master treat its servants?

9. In contrast, what kind of Master is God to His servants?

QUESTIONS FOR GOD

10. *God, this earth feels so real and attractive. How can I learn to long more for You and Your heaven, which I've never seen?*

11. *Do I truly own my possessions, or do they own me? Might it be a little of both? Would I think and live differently if I stopped referring to them as "my" possessions and started calling them what they are— "Yours"?*

FOR MEDITATION AND MEMORIZATION

Then he said to them, "Watch out!
Be on your guard against all kinds of greed;
a man's life does not consist in the abundance of his possessions."

LUKE 12:15

FOR FURTHER DISCUSSION

1. What aspects of this world are most effective at luring your affections away from heaven? What methods have you used to combat this competition for your heart?
2. Brainstorm a few strategies for keeping the brevity of the "dot" and the unending length of the "line" more clearly and consistently in view.
3. Discuss a few popular TV, radio, or billboard ads, and analyze their messages. What is true in each one? What is false? What is the strategy used to sell you on the message?
4. How have you experienced the tyranny of material wealth as your master? What has been your experience of God as your Master?
5. What other roadblocks, besides those mentioned in this lesson, do you wrestle with as you grow in your giving? What Scripture passages might help us deal with them?

TREASURE NOW OR LATER?

Based on pages 56–61 of chapter 5, "Roadblocks to Giving,"
in *The Treasure Principle, Revised and Updated*

Our enemy would like us to waste our lives chasing after material wealth, as though it would last forever. God says material wealth has value for only a short time and that its value is limited. Start your study time now by praying for discernment between the devil's lies and God's truth.

CHASING THE WIND

You've played the game…imagining what you would do with unlimited wealth. A few people throughout history have had the opportunity to actually *live* it. One of them—Solomon—recorded his findings.

1. Read the quotations from some of the world's wealthiest people on page 54 of *The Treasure Principle, Revised and Updated*. What do they say that leaves an impression with you? (And how does it fit with the numerous studies showing that lottery winners are often less happy two years after winning the lottery than before?)

2. Put Solomon's conclusions about wealth (Ecclesiastes 2:10–11) into your own words.

> As the wealthiest man on earth, Solomon learned that affluence didn't satisfy. All it did was give him greater opportunity to chase more mirages. People tend to run out of money before mirages, so they cling to the myth that things they can't afford will satisfy them.

3. Read Ecclesiastes 5:10–15, along with Randy's paraphrases on pages 57–58 of *The Treasure Principle, Revised and Updated*. Choose one of Solomon's statements that has been especially evident in your experience. How does it help explain the emptiness of materialism?

THE ANTIDOTE TO MATERIALISM

> Why do we keep getting fooled? Because our hearts yearn for treasure here and now. We're tempted to imagine that the earthly treasures we see around us are the genuine items rather than mere shadows of the real treasures.

How can we combat the seductive illusions of earthly treasure? Treasure Principle Key #5 says, "Giving is the only antidote to materialism."

4. A. W. Tozer said: "Whatever is given to Christ is immediately touched with immortality." How would you handle your wealth differently if you fully believed this?

5. Virtually all of us in Western culture are wealthy by global standards, so 1 Timothy 6:17–19 is intended for our ears. Read it and describe in your own words the fruit that comes from our giving.

> The act of giving is a vivid reminder that it's all about God, not about us. It's saying I am not the point. *He* is the point. He does not exist for me. I exist for Him….
>
> When I give [something] away…the magic spell is broken. My mind clears, and I recognize God as owner, myself as servant, and other people as intended beneficiaries of what God has entrusted to me….
>
> Only giving breaks me free from the gravitational hold of money and possessions. Giving shifts me to a new center of gravity—heaven.

6. Think about your life and the specific ways you are lured by the dream world of materialism. How, exactly, does giving affect your material urges, both in the short run and in the long run?

We are all at various levels of "wakefulness," or awareness, of God's truth. Talk to your Father about the degree to which you are free from materialism's illusions and the degree to which you are still chasing the wind. Ask Him for wisdom to understand your own heart and for the life changes He desires.

CHASING WHAT TRULY COUNTS

Even many Christians have settled for a life of unsatisfying material acquisitions, like making mud pies in a slum.

There's something so much better than anything the world can offer—eternal treasures and exhilarating joy.

7. How would a worldly critic likely evaluate the worth of Paul's life pursuits in Philippians 3:12–14?

8. How would you answer this critic if you had the chance?

9. What tips does Hebrews 12:1–2 provide to help us run our race well? (The "witnesses" refer to the Old Testament heroes of faith listed in Hebrews 11.)

10. What true wealth does God promise in Revelation 3:17–18 in exchange for the material treasures we give to Him? What do the gold, white clothes, and salve symbolize in spiritual reality?

QUESTIONS FOR GOD

11. *God, help me find encouragement in the ways I have been investing my life and my resources for eternal value. Then help me to see the ways I have been chasing the wind—and help me to repent of them and find the joy of following Your path instead.*

12. *God, what is Your attitude toward me after all the opportunities I've squandered (read 1 John 1:7, 9 as you ponder God's response)?*

FOR MEDITATION AND MEMORIZATION

Command them to do good, to be rich in good deeds,

and to be generous and willing to share.

In this way they will lay up treasure for themselves

as a firm foundation for the coming age,

so that they may take hold of the life that is truly life.

1 TIMOTHY 6:18–19

FOR FURTHER DISCUSSION

1. Let's put ourselves in Solomon's sandals (which would far outclass Guccis). Discuss what he must have had to go through in order to come to the point of weary emptiness in Ecclesiastes 2:10–11.
2. Which illusions of material wealth are most likely to fool you? Which realities of heavenly wealth have been most encouraging to you?
3. Tell about a time when giving helped you "wake up" to the realities of earthly and heavenly treasure.
4. What more can we learn from 1 Corinthians 9:24–27 and 2 Timothy 4:7–8 about how to chase after what truly matters?
5. How can we help each other run the race well rather than stopping or going off course?

LEARNING TO GIVE

Based on pages 62–70 of chapter 6, "Getting Started,"
in *The Treasure Principle, Revised and Updated*

Giving is a skill. And just as with any other skill in our lives, it must be learned. You may already be adept at giving, or you may still be developing the talent. In any case, God assures us that we will find fulfillment as we "excel in this grace of giving" (2 Corinthians 8:7). Ask your Father to take you to the next step.

GIVING 101

Under the First Covenant, the Israelites actually paid three required tithes, for an annual average of 23 percent. This total went toward three purposes—civil government, spiritual leadership, and caring for the poor. So we can't make an exact comparison, but the tithe that went to the priests and temple may be analogous to supporting our churches and pastors today. Randy writes,

> I have mixed feelings [about teaching that tithing is our starting point today]. I detest legalism. I certainly don't want to try to pour new wine into old wineskins, imposing superseded First Covenant restrictions on Christians. Every New Testament example of giving goes far beyond the tithe. However, none falls short of it.

Randy recognizes that tithing has been misused and misrepresented but still believes we should consider it as a logical starting point of giving, the training wheels that can get us going. You need to decide before God whether you agree, but try to withhold your judgment until you've finished the lesson.

1. Here are a few key passages helpful in guiding New Covenant believers (us) as we think about the First Covenant law. What principles can you draw from them as you seek to apply God's Word to your giving?

   • Matthew 5:17–20

   • Matthew 9:10–17

   • Matthew 13:52

   • Galatians 3:17–25

   • Jeremiah 31:31–34; Hebrews 8:6–13

It seems fair to ask, "God, do You really expect less of me—who has Your Holy Spirit within and lives in the wealthiest society in human history—than You demanded of the poorest Israelite?"...

Tithing isn't the ceiling of giving; it's the floor. It's not the finish line of giving; it's just the starting blocks. Tithes can be the training wheels to launch us into the mind-set, skills, and habits of grace giving.

2. As you contemplate Scripture's teaching, as well as Randy's comments, what is God telling you about your giving?

If God convicts you, take it seriously. The purpose of this self-examination is not to burden you with guilt, but to free you to live *without* guilt, which requires coming to terms with true guilt and confessing it. The goal is that we might please God and have the burdens of materialism lifted from our shoulders.

3. How would you respond if someone said to you, "There's no way I can give away 10 percent of my income. It's impossible!"? Besides asking, "If your income dropped by 10 percent, would you die?" what else might you say?

GRADUATE LEVEL GIVING

Under the First Covenant, once an Israelite had paid his required tithes, he often gave additional freewill offerings to God.

> Malachi says that the Israelites robbed God by withholding not only their mandatory tithes but also their voluntary "offerings." By giving less in their freewill offerings than He expected of them, they were robbing God. If they could rob God with insufficient freewill offerings, can't we do the same today?

4. What does each of the following passages teach regarding our freewill giving?

   • Malachi 3:8

   • Mark 12:41–44

   • Acts 4:34–5:10

   • 2 Corinthians 8:1–5

   • 2 Corinthians 9:6–8

   • 2 Corinthians 9:13 (note "obedience" here)

5. Recall from lesson 3 that God is the owner of all we possess and we are His stewards, or managers. Why is this important to remember as we consider our level of voluntary giving?

Talk with your Father about all He has generously entrusted to you, both for your enjoyment and for His kingdom purposes. Ask Him for the freedom to think and live strategically, caring for your family's needs but not saying yes to every want, freeing up God's funds to give more generously.

GOD'S CLASSROOM

Tithing is like a toddler's first steps: They aren't his last or best steps, but they're a good start. Once you learn to ride a bike, you don't need the training wheels. Once you learn to give, tithing becomes irrelevant. And if you can ride the bike without ever using training wheels, good for you....

Like piano playing, giving is a skill. With practice, we get better at it. We can learn to give more, give more often, and give more strategically. We teach the pursuit of excellence in our vocations. Why not make giving something we study, discuss, and sharpen, striving for excellence?

6. How might you go about training your heart to...

   • "excel in this grace of giving" (2 Corinthians 8:7)?

   • cultivate the faith that gives beyond your ability (8:3)?

   • give eagerly, not under compulsion (9:7)?

God must be a partner with you in all of these aspects of spiritual growth. You can't do any of them alone. Consider carefully how He, and fellow believers, can play a role in your learning process.

QUESTIONS FOR GOD

7. *God, search my heart and show me whether I'm allowing any excuses to hold me back from the joy and fulfillment of giving generously. Give me the wisdom to discern between an excuse and a valid doctrinal position.*

8. *God, if I've been robbing You—by withholding the tithe or the freewill offerings You want me to give—how do You feel toward me (consider 1 John 1:7, 9)? What do You want me to do next?*

FOR MEDITATION AND MEMORIZATION

But just as you excel in everything—

in faith, in speech, in knowledge,

in complete earnestness and in your love for us—

see that you also excel in this grace of giving.

2 CORINTHIANS 8:7

FOR FURTHER DISCUSSION

1. Let's talk openly about the pros and cons of various viewpoints about tithing for New Testament believers. Let's go into the discussion with a willingness to hear and understand even the positions we might disagree with. We'll stop the discussion if defenses start to rise.

2. Regardless of where you stand on tithing, why do you think most believers don't live by the dominant principle of generous freewill giving, which will lead only to greater joy and fulfillment (Acts 20:35)?

3. What has worked (or not worked) as you've grown in the skill of giving?

4. Should prayer warriors tell us nothing about their prayer lives and Bible students nothing about how they study the Bible? While respecting others' privacy, how can we encourage each other toward more mature giving? How can skilled givers pass on what they've learned without being prideful?

_____

GOOD QUESTION...

Based on pages 71–82 of chapter 6, "Getting Started,"
in *The Treasure Principle, Revised and Updated*

In this lesson we'll examine in greater depth three practical questions about giving. Invite your Father to open your mind and heart to whatever He wants to show you. You can trust Him.

GIVE IT NOW OR GIVE IT LATER?

People ask, "Should I give now, or should I hang on to it, hoping my investments will do well and I'll have more to give in a year or two?"

I respond with two questions of my own: "How soon do you want to experience God's blessing?" and "Do you want to be sure the money goes to God's kingdom, or are you willing to risk that it won't?"

1. What would James say about plans to give away money in the future, but not today (James 4:13–17)?

2. Since your heart goes where you put God's money, will withholding from giving now make you more or less inclined to give later? Explain.

I don't believe it's ever wrong to give now. With 10,000 percent interest (Matthew 19:29), God can produce far greater returns on money invested in heaven today than Wall Street or real estate ever can....

Death isn't your best opportunity to give; it's the end of your opportunity to give. God rewards acts of faith done while we're still living.

3. List one or two giving dreams you would like to achieve for God, in His strength, before your life is over.

What Will We Leave the Kids?

It's natural for parents to desire that their children, of all ages, are well cared for. But...

I've heard countless inheritance horror stories over the years. Study the lives of people who have inherited significant wealth and you'll find that in the vast majority of cases, it's made them more unhappy, greedy, and cynical.... Leaving more to God's kingdom and less to financially independent children is not just an act of love toward God, but toward them.

4. Biblical culture, in which an inheritance of land and house was essential to keep adult children from poverty, was radically different than ours today. When children are grown and financially independent, what can happen, positively and negatively, when they receive a windfall from their parents' estate?

5. How can you leave enough to your children to help them, but not enough to hurt or tempt them? How might the difference benefit God's kingdom?

6. Randy says that what our children need most from us is a heritage, not an inheritance. Think of a few spiritual "assets" you want to leave your children when your life is over. How can you start this week? (Ask the Lord for insight.)

WHY HAS GOD ENTRUSTED SO MUCH TO US?

Treasure Principle Key #6 says: "God prospers me not to raise my standard of living, but to raise my standard of giving."

Why does God give some of His children more than they need and others less than they need? So that He may use His children to help one another. He doesn't want us to have too little or too much (Proverbs 30:8–9). When those with too much give to those with too little, two problems are solved. When they don't, two problems are perpetuated.

7. Consider the FedEx delivery analogy (*The Treasure Principle, Revised and Updated,* 79). If you lived by the following Scripture passages, how would you handle wealth beyond what you need?

   • 2 Corinthians 8:14–15

   • 2 Corinthians 9:10–11

8. Think about the early Jerusalem believers who enthusiastically lived out this principle (Acts 2:44–45; 4:33–37). To whom might you minister with your excess wealth?

9. Where is the line between necessity and excess? What do you really need, and what can you give away? Are the answers different for different people? Take some time to talk with your Father about this. Return to these questions over the next several days.

When God provides more money, we often think, *This is a blessing.* Well, yes, but it would be just as scriptural to think, *This is a test.*

10. We usually apply the message of James 1:2–4 to hardships. But how might excess wealth *also* serve as a test to demonstrate our true values and strengthen our faith?

QUESTIONS FOR GOD

11. *God, is there really any danger in giving too much too soon? Or is the real danger in waiting too long? How much would I have to give away before I actually became irresponsible (consider Mark 12:41–44)?*

12. *Your Word gives me the basic principles, but the particulars of timing, inheritance, and other giving issues are harder to figure out. How can I discern Your wisdom from among all the voices around me...friends, family, church, the needy, financial counselors, and so on?*

FOR MEDITATION AND MEMORIZATION

You will be made rich in every way

so that you can be generous on every occasion,

and through us your generosity

will result in thanksgiving to God.

2 CORINTHIANS 9:11

FOR FURTHER DISCUSSION

1. Which risks are most likely to arise if you wait to give? How can you avoid them?
2. Looking ahead to your children's inheritance, what blend of material and spiritual wealth do you think will best serve them? How can you prepare your children for their *real* inheritance?
3. How have you seen God fulfill His promises from Malachi 3:10 and Luke 6:38?

Lesson 12

CATCH THE VISION

Based on pages 83–92 of chapter 7, "For Such a Time As This,"
in *The Treasure Principle, Revised and Updated*

As we near the end of our study, it's time to bring to bear all we've learned about our present and future opportunities. Ask your Father to fill you with anticipation for the adventure ahead—both for the rest of your earthly life and for your life forever in heaven.

Declaring heaven as your destination assumes that you're a child of God through faith in Christ—but that's something you should know for sure, not just assume! If you're not sure, ask a committed Christian friend to help you become sure. God says we can be certain of our eternal destination (1 John 5:13).

VIEWING LIFE FROM THE END

Five minutes after we die, we'll know exactly how we should have lived. But God has given us His Word so we don't have to wait to die to find out. And He's given us His Spirit to empower us to live that way now.

1. Write the obituary you hope will be printed after your life has ended. Focus on aspects of your character, your acts of obedience, and your influence on others, including your giving.

2. How would you answer these questions from *The Treasure Principle*: *"Five minutes after I die, what will I wish I would have given away while I still had the chance?* When you come up with an answer, why not give it away now? Why not spend the rest of our lives closing the gap between what we'll wish we would have given and what we really are giving?"

> **We have one brief opportunity—a lifetime on earth—to use our resources to make a difference.**

3. What steps might God be prompting you to take during the next few weeks as you grow in your giving and as you influence other people's attitudes toward giving?

A Historic Opportunity

There has never been a time of such affluence as in our culture today—nor a time of such need, materially and spiritually.

> Just as Esther [see Esther 4:14] was in a position of privilege, so is nearly everyone reading this book. Are you educated and literate? Do you have food, clothing, shelter, a car, perhaps some electronic equipment? Then you are among the privileged, the world's wealthy.

4. How does it affect your sense of responsibility and opportunity to recognize your true wealth?

5. Guilt is a natural response to these insights. How can you convert guilt into positive, action-oriented motivation (consider 1 John 1:7, 9; 1 Peter 1:13; John 15:5–8)?

6. Romans 12:6–8 lists "giving" among the spiritual gifts. Why do you think this spiritual gift is so seldom discussed? Why might God widely distribute the gift of giving among believers in affluent cultures today (*The Treasure Principle, Revised and Updated,* 86–87)?

7. As with most gifts, the gifted person excels in an area of obedience that applies to all believers. For example, all those without the gift of mercy are called to be merciful. Even if you don't have the gift of giving, how can you, empowered by God's Spirit, raise the level of your giving?

THE LEGACY WE LEAVE

When it comes to giving, churches operate under a
"don't ask, don't tell" policy. We lack communication,
accountability, and modeling. It's as if we have an
unspoken agreement: "I won't talk about it if you won't,
so we can go right on living as we are."

Think about it. How does a young Christian in the
church learn to give? Where can he go to see what giving
looks like in the life of a believer captivated by Christ?
Why are we surprised when, seeing no other example, he
takes his cues from a materialistic society?

8. Cultural expectations—such as our taboo about discussing a person's money—count for something. But when they hinder
obedience to God, we must rethink them. How can you, your family, and your fellow church members remain reasonably respectful
of each other's privacy while also modeling and sharing about
healthy giving in order to encourage and teach each other
(Hebrews 10:24)?

Unless we learn how to humbly tell each other our giving
stories, our churches will not learn to give.

9. Who are some people whose example could teach you about giving? Whom might you be able to encourage by your example
(Matthew 5:16)? How will you make one or two of these connec-
tions?

10. How can you train generous givers within your own family?

QUESTIONS FOR GOD

11. *God, I'm catching the vision! How can I sustain it? How can I avoid the distractions that threaten to keep me from seeing my life from eternity's perspective?*

12. *There are so many needs! Which ones do You intend as the recipients of the excess wealth You are entrusting to my care?*

FOR MEDITATION AND MEMORIZATION

And let us consider how we may spur one another

on toward love and good deeds.

HEBREWS 10:24

FOR FURTHER DISCUSSION

1. How can we help each other maintain perspective and take action in the face of the world's overwhelming need?
2. When it comes to our giving, where is the balance between respecting privacy and avoiding pride *and* obeying God's instruction to let our lights shine and to "spur one another on toward love and good deeds"?
3. Let's focus on each group member for a minute and dream together about how God might use his or her giving for His kingdom. None of the ideas we share are shackles to restrict one's direction, only possibilities.
4. If you're planning some new step in giving, how can we support and encourage you? How can we pray?

PREPARE FOR ACTION

Based on pages 92–100 of chapter 7, "For Such a Time As This,"
in *The Treasure Principle, Revised and Updated*

If God has been moving your heart, you may already be changing your thinking and habits about money and giving. It's time now to solidify plans for your next steps of giving maturity. But no efforts will succeed without Jesus Christ's involvement (John 15:5). Invite Him to guide your plans.

1. Consider the excerpts about the transformed Scrooge from the end of Dickens's *A Christmas Carol* (*The Treasure Principle*, 92–94). How does the prospect of a life focused more on giving than on keeping appeal to you?

THOUGHTS TO CONSIDER

Consider the following questions, which are intended to help you clarify your giving plan. Write your thoughts about each question that applies. You may need to ponder some questions for a few days or talk them over with family.

2. How am I doing at my basic giving commitment to God, beginning with my local church (1 Corinthians 9:9–12; Galatians 6:6)? Whether I believe in the 10 percent guideline or not, do I qualify as a true giver?

3. How much is God leading me to give in freewill offerings? Where should I give them? (Since each person's answers are different, ask God for wisdom [James 1:5].)

4. How strategic or worthy are the organizations or individuals I'm supporting or considering supporting? Do I know and agree with their values and purposes? Does God agree with them? (See Randy Alcorn's "Nineteen Questions to Ask Before You Give to Any Organization" at https://www.epm.org/resources/2012/Dec/26/nineteen-questions-ask-you-give-any-organization/.)

5. To whom might I pass along what I've learned about the Treasure Principle? How could I do this—through the book, prayer, a Bible study or discussion group, or other study materials?

MY GIVING COVENANT

Now for your plan of action:

6. Consider each commitment in the Giving Covenant (*The Treasure Principle, Revised and Updated,* 94–96, 101), and jot down a thought or two about what it will mean to implement it in your life. Does it require you to change any habits or thinking? How might accountability relationships help you fulfill it? How might it affect your prayer focus?

   - *Commitment #1:* I affirm God's full ownership of me (1 Corinthians 6:19–20) and everything entrusted to me (Psalm 24:1).

   - *Commitment #2:* I will set aside the firstfruits—starting with at least 10 percent—of all I receive, treating it as holy and belonging exclusively to the Lord (Malachi 3:8–10).

   - *Commitment #3:* Out of the remaining treasures God entrusts to me, I will seek to make generous freewill gifts (2 Corinthians 9:11).

   - *Commitment #4:* I ask God to teach me to give sacrificially to His purposes, including helping the poor and reaching the lost (2 Corinthians 8:3).

   - *Commitment #5:* Recognizing that I cannot take earthly treasures from this world, I determine to lay them up as heavenly treasures—for Christ's glory and the eternal good of others and myself (Matthew 6:19–21).

- *Commitment #6:* I ask God to show me how to lead others to the present joy and future reward of the Treasure Principle (Hebrews 10:24).

THE GREATEST PLEASURE

Do you want to experience this kind of joy? I invite you to transfer your assets from earth to heaven. I invite you to give humbly, generously, and frequently to God's work. Excel in giving so that you may please God, serve others, and enjoy treasures in heaven.

I urge you to embrace Christ's invitation: "Give, and it will be given to you" (Luke 6:38). Then when He gives you more, remind yourself why: that you may be generous on every occasion.

I invite you to send your treasures on to heaven, where they will safely await you. When you do, you'll feel the freedom, experience the joy, and sense the smile of God.

7. What is your next step? What dreams might await you as you take that step?

When you give, you'll feel His pleasure.

QUESTIONS FOR GOD

8. *God, this is exciting, but also a little frightening. How can I continue to rest in Your strength and wisdom? How can I maintain confidence that You're there guiding me and protecting me as I seek to obey You?*

9. *Thank You, Father, for changing me! Give me the courage and vision to pass on my joy to someone else. Who might that be?*

FOR MEDITATION AND MEMORIZATION

"I am the vine; you are the branches.

If a man remains in me and I in him,

he will bear much fruit;

apart from me you can do nothing."

JOHN 15:5

FOR FURTHER DISCUSSION

1. Now that we have come to the end of this study, what unanswered questions remain? Can we as a group address some of them?
2. What emotional difficulties are some of us dealing with: fear, guilt, uncertainty? How can we encourage each other and pray for these needs?
3. What cause do we already have for celebration? What victories have already been won or are in progress in our lives? (Let's celebrate!)
4. What is the next step each of us plans to take? How can we support one another as we step forward in faith?
5. How will each of us ensure regular follow-up with one or more people, from this group or elsewhere, to keep us on the path of generous giving?

If you wish to study in depth the biblical teachings on finances, see Randy Alcorn's revised and updated stewardship classic, *Money, Possessions, and Eternity* (Wheaton, Ill.: Tyndale House Publishers, 2003).

Nonfiction titles from RANDY ALCORN

THE TREASURE PRINCIPLE:
Unlocking the Secret of Joyful Giving
Bestselling author Randy Alcorn uncovers the revolutionary key to spiritual transformation: joyful giving! Jesus gave his followers this life-changing formula that guarantees not only kingdom impact, but immediate pleasure and eternal rewards.

THE PURITY PRINCIPLE:
God's Safeguards for Life's Dangerous Trails
God has placed warning signs and guardrails to keep us from plunging off the cliff. Find straight talk about sexual purity in Randy Alcorn's one-stop handbook for you, your family, and your church.

THE GRACE AND TRUTH PARADOX:
Responding with Christlike Balance
Living like Christ is a lot to ask! Discover Randy Alcorn's two-point checklist of Christlikeness—and begin to measure everything by the simple test of grace and truth.

PROLIFE ANSWERS TO PROCHOICE ARGUMENTS
This revised and updated guide offers timely information and inspiration from a "sanctity of life" perspective. Real answers to real questions appear in logical and concise form.

Best-selling *Fiction* from Randy Alcorn

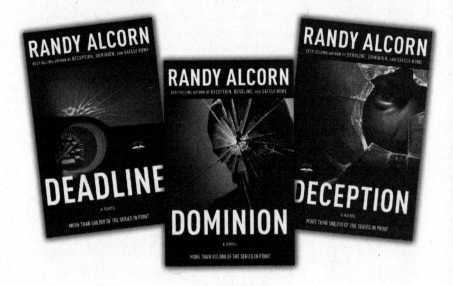

DEADLINE
After tragedy strikes those closest to him, journalist Jake Woods is drawn into a complex murder investigation that ultimately forces him to seek answers to the meaning of his existence.

DOMINION
When two murders drag a columnist into the world of gangs and racial conflict, Clarence Abernathy seeks revenge for the killings and answers to hard issues regarding race and faith.

DECEPTION
A jumbled mess of lies and secrets find Ollie Chandler investigating a perplexing, dangerous murder mystery. Bristling with tension and suspicion, *Deception* will take you to heaven and hell...and back again.

LORD FOULGRIN'S LETTERS

Foulgrin, a high-ranking demon, instructs his subordinate on how to deceive and destroy Jordan Fletcher and his family. It's like placing a bugging device in hell's war room, where we overhear our enemies assessing our weaknesses and strategizing attacks. *Lord Foulgrin's Letters* is a *Screwtape Letters* for our day, equally fascinating yet distinctly different—a dramatic story with earthly characters, setting, and plot. A creative, insightful, and biblical depiction of spiritual warfare, this book will guide you to Christ-honoring counterstrategies for putting on the full armor of God and resisting the devil.

RANDY ALCORN
MORE GREAT FICTION

THE ISHBANE CONSPIRACY

Jillian is picture perfect on the outside, but terrified of getting hurt on the inside. Brittany is a tough girl who trusts almost no one. Ian is a successful athlete who dabbles in the occult. And Rob is a former gangbanger who struggles with guilt, pain, and a newfound faith in God. These four college students will face the ultimate battle between good and evil in a single year. As spiritual warfare rages around them, a dramatic demonic correspondence takes place. Eavesdrop on the enemy, and learn to stave off your own defeat, in reading *The Ishbane Conspiracy*.